Threnody

Threnody

Juliet Patterson

NIGHTBOAT BOOKS
NEW YORK

ISBN: 978-1-937658-55-7

Design and typesetting by Mary Austin Speaker
Text set in Stempel Garamond

Cataloging-in-publication data is available from the Library of
Congress

Distributed by University Press of New England
One Court Street
Lebanon, NH 03766
www.upne.com

Nightboat Books
New York
www.nightboat.org

CONTENTS

I.

II.

III.

IV.

I

TOWARD

Toward a flower-
ing I came

lowly lupine raised
wrist

a loop of memory and its variable
eye

the deer coming closer—

Out of she
to you

how many sights
circle absence

the hollow and lake

how many transfigure
positioned against

the ear of my ear and the ghost
of the ear

THAT MUSIC

There were wars going on—

we were lying there

in the constant singing
of radios

lonely
a scant defense

reading our hands

as an eye going
upward

a house strictured
in rain

and August
sweat

~

Tourists, again

we're told it's a terror
of partly knowing

in all manner
words

and shapes

buds in the palm, say
or the red of two

mouths: marked by monuments

to an earlier idea

and stopped by nothing
stopping

~

Nights' flagellum: contact
mines,

shardsealed fields,
dull.

Upended, rice
edge of a house

by its scent, rubber
and dust

to your left /

down avenues where one
cannot speak.

~

What war?
We never heard.

Outside, the river's broken
murmur

faster, fast

and hewn, white
the sun

sprays of vegetation

your hand gathers
and the rain

you guess this time,
it's God.

SUMAC, WINTER RAIN

Seeded, a somewhere pulled
the veins

across ribs studded with berries
in the curved harbor

the letters of the words of our legs and arms
thin, pointed

each branch illustrating morning's profusion
waking a lamp, a scratch, a hole

the flat and empty landscape
on the far side

of the lake
where morning's ice lacquers that color

a wrist hoisted its ankles after
to forget the bombing

NOUNAL

Purblind wall-space, white

white, tree-studded

tract in the windowed

air. Ray of light points, the dark marsh

shows its way through

the ragged wood.

The half-opened door,

you, with all your otherness.

Here, the faint sounds

of shade, the tumbled sheen

of home. A wave, a word,

adrift.

Said, disappearing these

fingers will them-

selves of you into night.

Had through marsh fog

sculled down with the wind-shuttled

buds as against our erudition

of which flowers our nature

to vanish. In a small house

deeply the wooing that penetrated

to the sea returns to a breath-papered room

in green arms

and empty.

Figured the wide-open stretch of bay

flickered out against a life

given up to water.

Hand against a flight

of color, without a place

to rest in worked circles

of sound. Sand patterns

naked under dead leaves,

a gull sick with sun, pulled up on shore

by the whitest rationing,

the one we kept burying

and re-burying.

Future writ in white

spaces, wouldn't stop

the shelled meadow

holding morning's swell;

all its rolling loam, slow fracture

that if paraphrased

would set a pure interval

between us like a word

offered silently

and then returned

in order to disturb things

otherwise clear.

As against the water's

edging, thrashed

leaves, our knees tucked

under.

The wave-line on shell, sand, wall

pulled fingers and hair meshed

through pine. Limbs, limbs

the water's body shot,

into its dark vowel,

quavering. The wave,

through strung gutturals,

that uttered, not stillness,

said. In us, impulse testing

the unknown. What quickens:

clarity, the outline of a leaf and dull

window our mouths move

under. Through the glass

pane, how fast, the white dispatch

of gulls, disappearing in cracks

of the road.

II

WHITE CEDAR, MIGRATORY NOON

Cold and waxwings.
Waxwings in the
                    wind
cold some wild pole,
so sky then, new
of winter.

Cold around our arms
and primitive
touch; noon advancing
its flattened leaf

and quieter than that the waxwings
away from us
in the velocity of rest.

THRENODY

How the too-large body

and its futile vision

floods into bee-life

of wild buckthorn, clusters of white

blossoms, anthers bright.

Leaving from safety,

from the most living green

tip out into space,

each body, each thought

entering the solitary

center, hidden center, a flower

brims, nevertheless yes,

a little hole

in the eye.

So small a picture,

the blind pressure of smoke

splitting now in vacant

comb. So small, the bulk,

a handful of workers flaring the wooden sill,

whose substance, solid, whose life

burst furious through fields.

And the sights of time, the world's time

becoming completely destitute

time, but also perhaps not, not yet,

not even yet.

Of the hard grasses, reading

stations of the weed.

What light is like this?

What answers and rises

in our hand? The shimmering plain

half in, half out of time.

The field's effacement

into water, the flower heaving

the stone.

Half-glimpsed figure

in the flower image,

indweller

of the fullsacked center

where bright anthers

touch and touch distances

the bee begins.

Not of shadow,

but of light, unfolding

its wings, quits

its pediments to write

the prairie's simulacra,

a letter unreturned,

the dead, this time,

dead.

Little hole, the dead

in plural strokes of tweezers

pulled from capped broods,

callow bodies

in the turn of seasons

small terror in bright centuries,

here, smoke and glove

and the keeper drawing others,

annulled a lessening riot

of the hives' pitch,

the slant blade

unchaining, minutes

shaved, upthrust in wet mounts,

bodies jeweled in alcohol

tongueless in the yard

of clouds crushing quietly,

spring.

Chance and chance

all that is visible

moves the eye

and pierces or erodes

the mind's structure.

Everything moves

on, the heather, the clover,

the juniper bushes, cheat grass.

And into land: water, the river

running into sea, and the sea, open ocean

contracted by a time-scale

of exponential growth,

the hale and the whole, effaced

and on the silent coasts,

failed wings.

SUGAR MAPLE, WINTER DROUGHT

Flared plates of trunk, a foot stalk
with seed in its heart,

clear sap.
What thought burns here?

As if our quiet tomorrow
is caught in sensation

of the trace-root's
sugaring,

the simple fact
of some erosion

and ecology's abolition
thin and barren

in February's little
chrome.

SEED BED, QUIESCENCE

Of you, as form,
                so wound as where our words

gather possession.
As each repetition

would accrete the seed
through soil's rime.

Pierced and touched
the husk, as where at last

our acts accumulate
to rend time's violence

and suggest futurity,
the smallest of numbers.

CHLOROSIS

The grammatical alarm
of a field

'thrown into relief'
sallow blossom and sensations

for their stems, once fragrant
as the first path of a bee.

The yellow structures pulling through clouds

late in a sequence
broken, tension of broken

sunlight and touched.

Drought, a violent sentence
our weather began.

A silence that is strange
the sources

into which one cannot introduce
primitive discrepancies

or the blades speaking
in one voice: make my image

vendor of wildermass
let be

what is gone.

THAW

A thought interrupts.

River, blistering pine
and floss, splinters

its soft bristlecone
of touch, as before a vagrancy,

with its inevitability, why?
How different is this field

from the one I scratched yesterday
for you?

Our table is empty,
a spring curling pond

and the water advancing
away from us

apprehends a pure event
in which some flowers through snow

show survival's grimace,
swinging clusters of red.

Long shadow, etched
inscape: how all things

rejoice
in the age to come.

III

"You know how to interpret the appearance of the earth and the sky; but why do you not know how to interpret the present time?"

— LUKE 12:56

"in a dark time the eye begins to see"

— THEODORE ROETHKE

ECLOGUE

        'were words, passages we'd leave
ourselves for—barge'

moving in and out
at the darkened peripheries

of cities or an atom's parts

        'that deep vessel: flame to an irretrievable
focus'

dragging past us on its sad current

otherwise just the flower
of a hungry gull

on frost-stricken
water

                    the water in leafless winter, untold

truth in leafless water, body's man
or woman

untold, the thought of the body

ice-tipped branches, the water
like an engine

shoring up the world in that deep inaction

and clouds
in frenzied stillness

nailing nails in the air

                    whose profile in margin where
four windows hang

whose body

where light still glows through the iced-over
panes

whose face in profile

be engendered after our own

some power, secret, the trees

where there is nothing but the slightest smoke

in place of a hammer

                  either now or tomorrow or the day after that

is repetition another human gilding
of the inanimate

driving, as into an infinite—what?

                  roads, forks, leavings, traceries
animal tracks etched in snow

black artery leaping once more

through the snow-clad
town

the stillness of the tree through fissures of windows

morning's silence and apprehension
of color

the chance of the sparrow hawk lifting
in the margin

answer absent ourselves or risk not being

understood—

                                        fog and its useless currents

burgeoning language

at shoreline where trees too had their place and lost
before

to the snow's erudition
now tomorrow's ragged grove—

let loose from description

also the water

imagining its own
shed

a sentence drawn in metal silts

the body
a boat

that carried
the means of giving up and descent

flame cell and metal salts

the import and export
of our fathers

'half bullies, half tortured

soldiers'

consider their barren last vanishing

an epic of unevent—except to find the harbor
                    rimmed by swallows and canoes—

here, a cult of relics
and wings

hardly had a foothold—

once touched and worn—scurf, repetition,
tradition

to sail

into historical position, hands consuming
the current

with a list of needs and a memory

not for pleasure, to hear the cry

inside a small coil
of ice

'these awful errors of craft—

uncertainty how a nation should respond to violence—
made up for by an urgent sense of mission'

vine, out of what voices?

fumes, buds, hanging of what
dead injunction?

all our sweet purchases already starting
toward inversion

all matter draining from the gravitational field

'the days, the gilt paint
we call fear'

                              becomes the familiar return
of images

like water over terrain: a day slips

where we stand in a stranger's white acre
beyond pardon

                    small teeth are set deep

with the sifting noise of a wrist
on paper

truth this inhuman fixing and all the earth
a lens

distillate and vapor

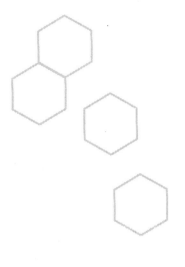

IV

DIMINISHED

the bees in thistle, where the throat burrs like something whispered

and the corollary—time—measured more greatly, cultivating

a language the random corrects. We like to hear the noise

of it, the self dividing word that pushes static

and furls its oath in the weights of earth

balance. There is something elemental

in our urgency; the hues through the nettles

and thorns, the cramped space of wings.

Is this God or another condition?

Beyond the limit of our word, a natural world; tense

and apprehensive.

EXTINCTION EVENT

To burst in your mind with costly grace.

To mass in your faceted syllables.

The arrested movement of time; hours
in clusters, overripe.

Hours, like broken offshoots,
flourishing as they can;

possibilities in sleeves of limitation.
Whorled taut, 'each brittle

node to a flushed
bud', last needles

embossed in clay.
That we break

from your tongue
and now tease ash,

stain of a titian
butterfly.

ELEGY

Someone's cutting with a chainsaw by water.

The sound of the machine rends its blade in air

that seizes and bends like a tongue probing the jaw's lonely holes.

When the work is done, everything falls silent.

By then, we are walking the lake's shore, slung with leaves,

thinking we might be grinding down

yesterday's grief in a crush of twigs

blunted like the end of a sentence. Where water swells

the sun's governance, a paragraph of wind.

Snow, falling so thinly now wakens and melts.

A frosted window's fern spray makes

our widowed skin.

So we might be freed from laying waste to darkness, we eat

the last of summer's raspberries from the freezer.

A longing for silence rushes in, and replaces for a moment

the darkness repeating its wish, coming as it does in the wake

of everything. Sunday flares up, a gall in memory

pungent in the spasm of fruit thinking who really survives

death? Snow falls. The lake clouds in a slurry of ice.

Our room shifts across the lake's surface, bright as bullet crystals

of snow as if the draft had used them for weeping.

The cold is early. Snow catches, star-shaped its leaves

and brightens into branches, rounding a new dark

and retrenching, repeating itself, as if elegy

were endless. The month gone and the day

coming up in blunt regions of the mind; words in the mouth

the way a mouth is wound, thinking none know death

but the living alone.

LITTORAL

Now: the canted tract of what nature elects—

what the eye, wedging, jams: scallops clamped
in the crude heave of wave

and its countless facets—
image where we lean
in again

~

There's beauty in what clings—

the sea lavender's prop
and body's toil

moving, at their restless extremity
forward

and the flattened fronds of sea-
mats

evince the eye and communion
it takes

~

Who is that nature of ours?

To say it, there is something to name

where the wave slides
                              its last edges

(spindles, whelks, loosened
coral)

                              to catch a figment, ripe

to feel the vacancy
              also —

REFUGIUM

Where wild, unkempt rays
quivered in the grove

measureless enough
and as you've just said,

deferred. Relict brake here
that uttered,

welled some hollow; pines
dismembering

as if each turgid node
might blossom

and bring, would bring
us as offering,

barter, the armament
and image

of the spray
and spore.

DARK SCAFFOLDING

Pushed through our window, the sunlight

shards evergreen and then this room, seizes

the heart because the eye has chosen it

and disappears with a rake of cloud.

From our small bed, the ocean is an eternity

contesting morning's full horizon; nothing but it

to see. Caught under tongue, waves grope

in time. They say, erased. Our eyes

have already seen all they can today

and escape as a finch throats invisible song

while you try to measure its skin through the curtain's

attenuation before, in your mind, it ascends.

Is nature a day begun?

I'm sorry I don't want words to wake me.

The swarm suspended near the door bursts

from your sleeve like a small resurrection

in the dwindling backdrop of sea.

The bees, dull with fatigue, flame your wrist

and draw light in a point of being, afraid

of the slur in July wind. How can it be spoken?

What's remade when the morning

beats us apart. The fray of wilderness

replaced with this itinerate hive

spread across the body's intractable

screen. The ocean: raw, sick and hot.

The bees causing you to admit your own

happiness.

Remember beauty?

The wild violets blooming too early

and the last word we heard lifting from the shadow's

range: coming up to away: a limit.

Winters without snow. Is this how

we'll remember it? The dune pained in blossom, a gesture

erasing silence whose message embraces

its quick in shifting pins that break

grasses into water into gutterings.

Cold, the morning. No wind.

'Branches motionless, dark

scaffolding made against the beach.'

Things have already happened

before we were here. That was now.

The weather suggests it's late

afternoon, waves crashing the air

tight. There are empty hands intervening

and a crowd gathered near a whale

on the beach. There, we wash in water

of odd names where a shallow cut lets blood

bead at the tip of the syringe. We advance, holding

hands as a knife ribbons the jaw and loosens

hemorrhaged tissue, against sand.

Soon the eye flushed, ferns every edge; carnelian,

rust, staining the throat's white pleats. The body's fin

hulking, colossal against fingers, animal curtaining

each blunt wave as in land, hand of roses

opening: the way of blood in water.

A tincture of wind and its nothing else

scored with sun's conjecture, a tidewash

of punctures in sand. And here is the ledge: fractured glint

and water beneath; slow roll of bees biting empty air.

Arm and leg, socket and joint, stiff words beneath

the skin rising to mind's casement, enclosing a right

of way. Anywhere, anywhere. The drift

and slip of body along shoreline's seam

unlocked to day's heat retracks the ringing

tide. We press our face to its changing ink; cluster

and drone, a blindsight to listening.

RETURN

to watch
a great deal of elsewhere

inhabiting the shore

mute, but implicative
as flowers

struggling at our feet

beachgrass

trapping a forgotten
hand

~

How something dies out
in us: the conversation, the hour

made out of nothing
but relationships

of again

as faint as the place where one
unhinges

its hope, I thought
the sea

~

O, beautiful
whale, say, calving

the one to draw
as we drown

filing the water's tongue

you know: the leap
goes over you, always

'not stillness' said, but the movement
traced, scattered

'black verse
the turn and the turn'

~

What's below us

the wave-belly

lovely

singly
suspended

fingering walls

in speech we wish to join
again

out of context

~

June June
like like

it then

unhoused palm in the sky
cold

then waves
bending

guttered strip

of beach

flee, you say

of again a winter

and hours destroyed
as moving

NOTES

"That Music"—"the constant singing of radios," –George Oppen, "A Narrative"

"White Cedar, Migratory Noon" takes part of its title from Joseph Ceravalo

"Threnody"—after Colony Collapse Disorder (CCD), a poorly understood phenomena in which bees from a beehive abruptly disappear. In six years, leading up to 2013, more than 10 million beehives were lost to CCD. Several possible causes have been suggested; no single proposal has gained widespread acceptance among the scientific community, but a 2014 Harvard study fingers the neonicotinoid class of pesticides as the key driver of the disease.

"Eclogue"—"were words, entire passages we'd leave / ourselves for—'barge'," and "that deep vessel: flame to an irretrievable /focus"—Gustaf Sobin, *Along America's Edge*

"half bullies, half tortured soldiers"—Inger Christensen, *alphabet*

"these awful errors of craft/uncertainty how a nation should respond to violence" and "an urgent sense of mission,"—Piotr Sommer, "Liberation in Language"

"the gilt paint we call fear"—Bei Dao, "Writing a Letter"

"Extinction Event" — "each brittle node to flushed bud" is adapted from Gustaf Sobin

"Dark Scaffolding" — The bodies of three blue whales washed ashore off the Southern California Coast within a two-week period in September 2007. Blue whale strandings are extremely uncommon. The title of this poem and the phrase "dark scaffolding made against the beach" comes from Rosmarie Waldrop.

"Return" — "black verse/the turn and turn" — George Oppen, *Selected Prose, Daybooks, and Papers*

ACKNOWLEDGMENTS

Grateful acknowledgment is made to the editors and readers of the following publications where some of these poems have appeared:

26 ("Sumac, Winter Rain," "Toward," as "Approaching a Scenic View"); *Connotation Press: An Online Artifact* ("Seed Bed, Quiescence," and "Thaw"); *Crazyhorse* ("Extinction Event"); *Pebble Lake Review* ("Nounal"); *Kissed By Venus* ("Diminshed," "Elegy" and one section from "Dark Scaffolding" — "Remember Beauty"); *Pistola* ("Chlorosis," Littoral," "White Cedar, Migratory Noon"); *Redivider* (two sections from "Dark Scaffolding" — "The weather suggests it's late" and "A tincture of wind and its nothing else"); *Sink Review* ("Refuguim," Return," "Sugar Maple, Winter Drought"); *Swerve* ("Eclogue"); *Water~Stone Review* ("That Music") and *WinteRed Press* ("Threnody")

Thanks to Jim Moore, William Stobb, Rebecca Wee, and Jan Weismiller for invaluable editorial assistance and support.

To Chris Baeumler, Jil Evans and Wendy Lewis. Perfect readers.

Thank you Lindsey Boldt and Mary Austin Speaker for your artistry and know-how.

Thank you, Kazim Ali and Stephen Motika.

Thank you, Olga Broumas.

And thank you as ever, Rachel Moritz.

JULIET PATTERSON is the author of *The Truant Lover*, winner of the Nightboat Books Poetry Prize, and the chapbooks *Epilogue* and *Dirge*. As a community activist and artist, Patterson has worked on a number of collaborative projects related to place-making and the environment. She lives in Minneapolis with her partner and son.

NIGHTBOAT BOOKS

Nightboat Books, a nonprofit organization, seeks to develop
audiences for writers whose work resists convention
and transcends boundaries. We publish books rich with
poignancy, intelligence, and risk. Please visit our website,
www.nightboat.org, to learn about our titles and how you can
support our future publications.

The following individuals have supported the publication
of this book. We thank them for their generosity and
commitment to the mission of Nightboat Books:

Elizabeth Motika
Benjamin Taylor

In addition, this book has been made possible, in part, by
grants from The National Endowment for the Arts, and The
New York State Council on the Arts Literature Program.

State of the Arts
NYSCA

ART WORKS.

National
Endowment
for the Arts
arts.gov